A Pocketful Of Poems

Edited By Vicki Skelton

First published in Great Britain in 2020 by:

Young Writers
Remus House
Coltsfoot Drive
Peterborough
PE2 9BF
Telephone: 01733 890066
Website: www.youngwriters.co.uk

All Rights Reserved
Book Design by Ashley Janson
© Copyright Contributors 2020
Softback ISBN 978-1-80015-105-5

Printed and bound in the UK by BookPrintingUK
Website: www.bookprintinguk.com
YB0451AZ

FOREWORD

Dear Reader,

Are you ready to get your thinking caps on to puzzle your way through this wonderful collection?

Young Writers are proud to introduce our new poetry competition, *My First Riddle*, designed to introduce pupils to the delights of poetry. Riddles are a great way to introduce children to the use of poetic expression, including description, similes and expanded noun phrases, as well as encouraging them to 'think outside the box' by providing clues without giving the answer away immediately. Some pupils were given a series of riddle templates to choose from, giving them a framework within which to shape their ideas.

Their answers could be whatever or whoever their imaginations desired; from people to places, animals to objects, food to seasons. All of us here at Young Writers believe in the importance of inspiring young children to produce creative writing, including poetry, and we feel that seeing their own riddles in print will ignite that spark of creativity.

We hope you enjoy riddling your way through this book as much as we enjoyed reading all the entries.

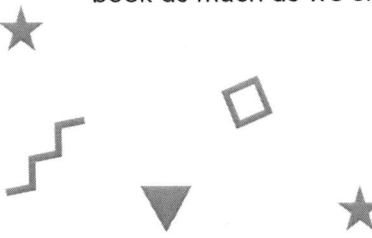

CONTENTS

Independent Entries

Zachary Hopper (5)	1
Ella Harwood (4)	2
Thomas Vilmos Anderson (4)	4
Anisa Sadikali (4)	6
Lottie Davies (5)	8
Mohammed Ayyub (5)	9
Zara Sarwar (5)	10
Zayaana Premji (5)	11
Georgina Valls-Russell (5)	12
Joel Robertson (5)	13
Gracie Ireland (5)	14
Emmy Egan	15
Ayaz Sadikali (7)	16
Devan Majithia (6)	17
Amélie Kotey (5)	18
Dylan Ennas	19
Vihaan Gada (3)	20
Alex Thompson (4)	21
Matthew Goble (5)	22
Alfie (4)	23
Sadie Pratt (2)	24
Umme-Hani Khan (4)	25
Jack Mason (4)	26
Aycha Ben-Saïd (4)	27
Isla Race (4)	28
Xander Bayley (5)	29
Lucy Penk (3)	30
Lewis Callaghan	31
Megan Harrigan	32
Willow Pidgeon (5)	33
Isaac Smith (9)	34
Dylan French (4)	35
Inan Kaya (2)	36
Dubem Nwogbo (4)	37
Zahra Ben-Saïd (5)	38
Alberta London (4)	39

Bangor Independent Christian School, Bangor

Lincoln Graham (4)	40

Brynford County Primary School, Brynford

Betsy Jones (5)	41

Castle Park Primary School, Caldicot

Elias Baker (5)	42
Renaee Boulasi (4)	43
Esme Harvey (5)	44
Gracie-May Bellamy (5)	45

Corpus Christi Primary School, Glasgow

Dylan Cook (5)	46

Croftcroighn School, Glasgow

Wayne Rwizi (11)	47
Charlie-Anne Bowes (10)	48
Gabriel Eghobamien (11)	49
James Barnes (9)	50
Lucas McGinley (8)	51

Gaelscoil Éadain Mhóir, Brandywell

Darragh Bradley (8)	52
Cayden Williams (8)	53
Michael Allen (7)	54
Ruairí Moore (7)	55
Caislín Clarke (9)	56
Killian Harkin (8)	57
Mia Pirone (8)	58

Harleston CE Primary Academy, Harleston

Amber Smithers (4)	59
Maxwell Aldred	60
Archie Cooper (5)	61

Killinchy Primary School, Killinchy

Ellie Robertson (6)	62
Zach Mitchell (5)	63
Noah Caughey (5)	64
Erin Shaw (4)	65
Freddy Hunniford (5)	66
Rosa Francis (5)	67
Will Agnew (5)	68
Daniel Gilmore (5)	69
Callum Wijkstra (5)	70
Maksis Briska-Emsins (5)	71
Molly Anderson (5)	72
Ollie Starbuck (5)	73
Eloise Reid (5)	74

Manley Park Primary School, Whalley Range

Felix Nicholson (4)	75
Maya Solomon-Thomas (5)	76
Tabitha Percy (5)	77
Sebastian Alton (5)	78
Benjamin McHague (4)	79
Agnes Oliveira (5)	80
Theo Nolan (5)	81
Sylvia Marshall (5)	82

Aoife Hodkinson (5)	83
Daisy Wild (4)	84
Zainab Zafar (5)	85
Silvie Naidu (5)	86
Rubi Alam (5)	87
William Stone (5)	88

Mullaglass Primary School, Newry

Jordi Marks (5)	89
Clara Jones (5)	90
Callum Marshall (5)	91
Cory Yates (5)	92
Oliver Patterson (5)	93
Emily Moffett (5)	94
Jack Laverty (5)	95
Jessica Copeland (6)	96
Poppy Baird (4)	97

Oakdale Primary School, Stanground

Olivia Boyden (5)	98
Harry Forth (5)	99
Jacob Silva-Banks (5)	100
Ashley Brighton (5)	101

Penybont Primary School, Bridgend

Adam Stajuda (4)	102
Ethan Mason (5)	103
Morgan Schokkenbroek (4)	104
Jasmine McLennon (5)	105
Leia Jury (4)	106
Reuben Hughes (5)	107
Esme Colwill Downs (5)	108
Joe Beckinsale (5)	109
Rex Carp (5)	110
Charlie Tunster-Price (5)	111
Reubin Fletcher (5)	112

Perry Hall Primary School, Wednesfield

Clara Eddies (4)	113
Ryley Redford	114
William Wilkinson (5)	115
Japji Shergill (5)	116
Lyla Gardner (5)	117
Holly Tanner (4)	118
Travis Scordis-Hutchinson (5)	119
Sebastian Smith (4)	120
Muhammad Masab (5)	121
Avneet Ghakal (5)	122
Jasleen Kahlon (4)	123
Harley Thomas (5)	124
Roop Sandhu (5)	125
Joshua Arrowsmith (4)	126
Mason Humpage (4)	127
Amara Summan (5)	128
Seth Brown (5)	129
Archie Marshall (4)	130
Demi-Leigh Davies (6)	131
Nishaan Kooner (5)	132
Aliyah Summan (5)	133
Sophia Hazell (5)	134
Logan Cooper (5)	135
Tyler Farnell (4)	136
Ekam Sekhon (5)	137
Hollie Webster (5)	138
Anayah Cadot (4)	139
Jenson Rogers (4)	140
Emilia Smith (5)	141
Evan Andrews (4)	142

St Fagans CW Primary School, Michaelston Super Ely

Mia Vatunitu (4)	143
Darren Martinson (4)	144
Phoebe Roberts (5)	145
Elliott Davey (4)	146
Ellis Dodd (5)	147
Willow Reddin (5)	148
Elsie Rhoden (5)	149

Sebastian Child (4)	150
Maddison Slack (5)	151
Mollie Waters (4)	152
Freya-L'ren Smith (5)	153
Lola (5)	154
Harry Winch (5)	155
Zara Gafuri (5)	156
Indigo Grant (4)	157

St Mungo's Primary School & Nursery Class, Glasgow

Antonina Krasuska (5)	158
Kye Chigwada (5)	159
Abdulaziz Othman (5)	160
Sarah Angela Reid (6)	161
Maria Alexandra Vargas Teixeira (5)	162
Cooper Mullan (6)	163
Lewis Hay (5)	164

Ysgol Bodafon, Llandudno

Henry Cogger (5)	165
Stori-Mae Paterson (5)	166
Layla Fairbairn-Percival (4)	167

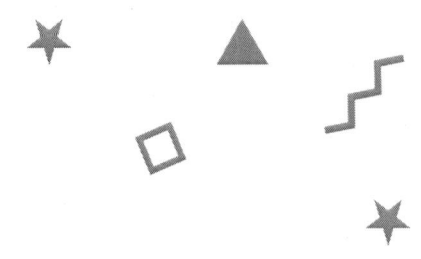

THE RIDDLES

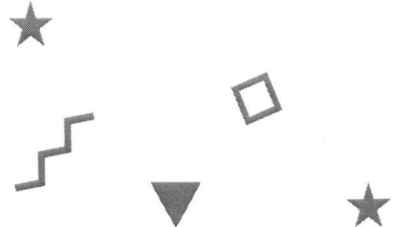

Zachary's First Riddle

This is my riddle about a fantastic person.
Who could it be? Follow the clues to see!

This person has **snowy white** hair,
Blue shirts are what they like to wear.
They like to watch **wildlife and plants** on TV,
And play **explorers** with me.
They like **chocolate** to eat,
And sometimes **ice cream** for a treat.
Travelling to see habitats is their favourite thing,
And **bird tweets** are what they sing.
The planet is their best friend,
And now this riddle is at the end.

Have you guessed who it could be?
Look below and you will see, it is...

Answer: David Attenborough.

Zachary Hopper (5)

Ella's First Riddle

This is my riddle about an amazing animal.
What could it be?
Follow the clues to see!

This animal has **brown shaped spots** on its body,
And its colours are **brown and beige**.
This animal has **four** feet,
It likes **green leaves from**
really tall trees to eat.
Africa and sometimes some zoos
are where it lives,
Its favourite thing to do is **walk around in big open spaces**.
This animal has **two furry** ears,
It makes **funny humming** sounds for you to hear.

Are you an animal whizz?
Have you guessed what it is?
It is...

Answer: A giraffe.

Ella Harwood (4)

Thomas' First Riddle

This is my riddle about an amazing animal.
What could it be?
Follow the clues to see!

This animal has **stripes** on its body,
And its colour is **orange to alarm everybody**.
This animal has **furry** feet,
It likes **fresh meat** to eat.
The jungle is where it lives,
Its favourite things to do are **hunt and eat**.
This animal has **spots on the back of its ears**,
It makes **roaring** sounds for you to hear.

Are you an animal whizz?
Have you guessed what it is?
It is...

Answer: A *tiger*.

Thomas Vilmos Anderson (4)

Anisa's First Riddle

This is my riddle about an amazing animal.
What could it be?
Follow the clues to see!

This animal has **a hump that looks like a mountain** on its body,
And its colour is **brown**.
This animal has **four** feet,
It likes **grass** to eat.
Desert is where it lives,
Its favourite thing to do is **bounce and take people for rides**.
This animal has **two** ears,
It makes **haa haa grunt** sounds for you to hear.

Are you an animal whizz?
Have you guessed what it is?
It is...

Answer: A camel.

Anisa Sadikali (4)

Lottie's First Riddle

What could it be?
Follow the clues and see.

It looks **yummy**.
It sounds **silent**.
It smells **sweet**.
It feels **spongy**.
It tastes **delicious**.

Have you guessed what it could be?
Look below and you will see,
It is...

Answer: A cupcake.

Lottie Davies (5)

Mohammed Ayyub's First Riddle

What could it be?
Follow the clues and see.

It looks **colourful and cubed**.
It sounds **chewy**.
It smells **like fruit**.
It feels **hard and soft**.
It tastes **yummy in my tummy**.

Have you guessed what it could be?
Look below and you will see,
It is...

Answer: Sweets.

Mohammed Ayyub (5)

Zara's First Riddle

What could it be?
Follow the clues and see.

It looks **orange and round**.
It sounds **squishy and crunchy**.
It smells **sweet and fresh**.
It feels **tough outside and soft inside**.
It tastes **yummy and juicy**.

Have you guessed what it could be?
Look below and you will see,
It is...

Answer: An orange.

Zara Sarwar (5)

Zayaana's First Riddle

What could it be?
Follow the clues and see.

It looks **white**.
It sounds **crunchy**.
It smells **of snow**.
It feels **cold**.
It tastes **of snow**.

Have you guessed what it could be?
Look below and you will see,
It is...

Answer: A snowman.

Zayaana Premji (5)

Georgina's First Riddle

What could it be?
Follow the clues and see.

It looks **black and white**.
It sounds **like squawks**.
It smells **icy**.
It feels **warm**.
It tastes **sour**.

Have you guessed what it could be?
Look below and you will see,
It is...

Answer: A penguin.

Georgina Valls-Russell (5)

Joel's First Riddle

What could it be?
Follow the clues and see.

It looks **big and watery**.
It sounds **splashy**.
It smells **of food**.
It feels **wet**.
It tastes **salty**.

Have you guessed what it could be?
Look below and you will see,
It is...

Answer: A water park.

Joel Robertson (5)

Gracie's First Riddle

What could it be?
Follow the clues and see.

It looks **like Happy Feet**.
It sounds **like barking**.
It smells **like water**.
It feels **fluffy**.
It tastes **cold**.

Have you guessed what it could be?
Look below and you will see,
It is...

Answer: A penguin.

Gracie Ireland (5)

Emmy's First Riddle

What could it be?
Follow the clues and see.

It looks **like a rocket**.
It sounds **crunchy**.
It smells **fruity**.
It feels **freezing cold**.
It tastes **icy and sweet**.

Have you guessed what it could be?
Look below and you will see,
It is...

Answer: *An ice lolly.*

Emmy Egan

Ayaz's First Riddle

This is my super first riddle.
What could it be?
Follow the clues to see!

A pencil case is where you'll find it,
It's made out of **wood**.
It is used for **writing**,
Its colour is **grey**.
It is a **long** shape,
It has **erasers**.

Have you guessed what it could be?
Look below and you will see,
It is...

Answer: A pencil.

Ayaz Sadikali (7)

Devan's First Riddle

What could it be?
Follow the clues and see.

It looks **yellow and spotty**.
It sounds **very quiet**.
It smells like **bark**.
It feels **furry and soft**.
It tastes like **leaves and branches**.

Have you guessed what it could be?
Look below and you will see,
It is...

Answer: A giraffe.

Devan Majithia (6)

Amélie's First Riddle

What could it be?
Follow the clues and see.

It looks **stripy**.
It sounds **noisy**.
It smells **like the flowers it sits on**.
It feels **painful if it stings you**.
It tastes **sweet to eat its honey**.

Have you guessed what it could be?
Look below and you will see,
It is...

Answer: A bee.

Amélie Kotey (5)

Dylan's First Riddle

This is my super first riddle.
What could it be?
Follow the clues to see!

Space is where you'll find it,
It's made out of **ice**.
It is used for **completing the solar system**,
Its colour is **blue**.
It is a **round shape** shape,
It has **a dark spot**.

Have you guessed what it could be?
Look below and you will see,
It is...

Answer: Neptune.

Dylan Ennas

Vihaan's First Riddle

This is my super first riddle.
What could it be?
Follow the clues to see!

The theatre is where you'll find it,
It's made out of **glass**.
It is used for **looking far, far away**,
Its colour is **red**.
It is a **1st round and 2nd round** shape,
It has **four circles**.

Have you guessed what it could be?
Look below and you will see,
It is...

Answer: *Binoculars*.

Vihaan Gada (3)

Alex's First Riddle

This is my super first riddle.
What could it be?
Follow the clues to see!

At a shop is where you'll find it,
It's made out of **hair and fur**.
It is used for **cuddling**,
Its colour is **blue**.
It is an **eight** shape,
It has **two eyes, one mouth, two arms and two legs**.

Have you guessed what it could be?
Look below and you will see,
It is...

Answer: A teddy bear.

Alex Thompson (4)

Matthew's First Riddle

What could it be?
Follow the clues and see.

It looks **green and white with a red laser.**
It sounds **like "To infinity and beyond."**
It smells **like greens.**
It feels **like plastic and its head is hard.**
It tastes **like plastic.**

Have you guessed what it could be?
Look below and you will see,
It is...

Answer: My Buzz Lightyear toy.

Matthew Goble (5)

Alfie's First Riddle

This is my riddle about an amazing animal.
What could it be?
Follow the clues to see!

This animal has **scales** on its body,
And its colour is **red**.
This animal has **little** feet,
It likes **fire** to eat.
A cave is where it lives,
Its favourite thing to do is **fly**.
This animal has **scaly** ears,
It makes **roaring** sounds for you to hear.

Are you an animal whizz?
Have you guessed what it is?
It is...

Answer: A dragon.

Alfie (4)

Sadie's First Riddle

This is my riddle about an amazing animal.
What could it be?
Follow the clues to see!

This animal has **spots** on its body,
And its colour is **red**.
This animal has **little** feet,
It likes **planets and insects** to eat.
Everywhere is where it lives,
Its favourite thing to do is **fly**.
This animal has **invisible** ears,
It makes **no** sounds for you to hear.

Are you an animal whizz?
Have you guessed what it is?
It is…

Answer: A ladybird.

Sadie Pratt (2)

Umme-Hani's First Riddle

This is my riddle about an amazing animal.
What could it be?
Follow the clues to see!

This animal has **a coat** on its body,
And its colours are **brown, white and orange**.
This animal has **paws for** feet,
It likes **meat** to eat.
Africa is where it lives,
Its favourite thing to do is **running**.
This animal has **small** ears,
It makes **roar** sounds for you to hear.

Are you an animal whizz?
Have you guessed what it is?
It is...

Answer: A lion

Umme-Hani Khan (4)

Jack's First Riddle

This is my riddle about an amazing animal.
What could it be?
Follow the clues to see!

This animal has **black spots** on its body,
And its colour is **white**.
This animal has **four huge** feet,
It likes **grass** to eat.
On a farm is where it lives,
Its favourite thing to do is **munch on grass**.
This animal has **sticky-out** ears,
It makes **moo** sounds for you to hear.

Are you an animal whizz?
Have you guessed what it is?
It is...

Answer: A cow.

Jack Mason (4)

Aycha's First Riddle

This is my riddle about an amazing animal.
What could it be?
Follow the clues to see!

This animal has **stripes** on its body,
And its colour is **orange and black**.
This animal has **four** feet,
It likes **meat** to eat.
The zoo is where it lives,
Its favourite thing to do is **sleep**.
This animal has **two** ears,
It makes **roar** sounds for you to hear.

Are you an animal whizz?
Have you guessed what it is?
It is...

Answer: A tiger.

Aycha Ben-Saïd (4)

Isla's First Riddle

This is my riddle about an amazing animal.
What could it be?
Follow the clues to see!

This animal has **a long neck** on its body,
And its colours are **yellow and brown**.
This animal has **four** feet,
It likes **leaves** to eat.
Africa is where it lives,
Its favourite thing to do is **eat from trees**.
This animal has **little** ears,
It makes **munching** sounds for you to hear.

Are you an animal whizz?
Have you guessed what it is?
It is...

Answer: A giraffe. (shown upside down)

Isla Race (4)

Xander's First Riddle

This is my riddle about an amazing animal.
What could it be?
Follow the clues to see!

This animal has **fur** on its body,
And its colours are **black and white**.
This animal has **four big** feet,
It likes **bamboo shoots and leaves** to eat.
China is where it lives,
Its favourite thing to do is **play**.
This animal has **two cute** ears,
It makes **growling** sounds for you to hear.

Are you an animal whizz?
Have you guessed what it is?
It is...

Answer: A panda.

Xander Bayley (5)

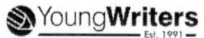

Lucy's First Riddle

This is my riddle about an amazing animal.
What could it be?
Follow the clues to see!

This animal has **a collar** on its body,
And its colours are **black and white**.
This animal has **four** feet,
It likes **sausages** to eat.
A house is where it lives,
Its favourite thing to do is **go for a long walk**.
This animal has **two** ears,
It makes **woof, woof** sounds for you to hear.

Are you an animal whizz?
Have you guessed what it is?
It is...

Answer: A sheep doggy.

Lucy Penk (3)

Lewis' First Riddle

This is my riddle about an amazing animal.
What could it be?
Follow the clues to see!

This animal has **feathers** on its body,
And its colour is **orange**.
This animal has **two** feet,
It likes **seeds** to eat.
The farm is where it lives,
Its favourite thing to do is **lay eggs**.
This animal has **no** ears,
It makes **cluck** sounds for you to hear.

Are you an animal whizz?
Have you guessed what it is?
It is...

Answer: A chicken.

Lewis Callaghan

Megan's First Riddle

This is my riddle about a fantastic person.
Who could it be? Follow the clues to see!

This person has **black** hair,
Dresses are what they like to wear.
They like to watch **movies** on TV,
And play **puzzles** with me.
They like **chicken** to eat,
And sometimes **ice cream** for a treat.
Singing is their favourite thing,
And **gospel music** is what they sing.
Dad is their best friend,
And now this riddle is at the end.

Have you guessed who it could be?
Look below and you will see, it is...

Answer: My mum.

Megan Harrigan

Willow's First Riddle

This is my riddle about a fantastic person.
Who could it be? Follow the clues to see!

This person has **neatly brushed** hair,
Cool clothes are what they like to wear.
They like to watch **anything** on TV,
And play **Lego** with me.
They like **burgers** to eat,
And sometimes **ice cream** for a treat.
Rugby is their favourite thing,
And **lovely songs** are what they sing.
Willow is their best friend,
And now this riddle is at the end.

Have you guessed who it could be?
Look below and you will see, it is...

Answer: Daddy.

Willow Pidgeon (5)

Isaac's First Riddle

This is my riddle about a fantastic person.
Who could it be? Follow the clues to see!

This person has **black** hair,
A blue jumper is what they like to wear.
They like to watch **cartoons** on TV,
And play **tickle** with me.
They like **apples** to eat,
And sometimes **chocolate** for a treat.
Dancing is their favourite thing,
And **Twinkle Star** is what they sing.
My mum is their best friend,
And now this riddle is at the end.

Have you guessed who it could be?
Look below and you will see, it is...

Answer: Aunty Michelle.

Isaac Smith (9)

Dylan's First Riddle

This is my riddle about a fantastic person.
Who could it be? Follow the clues to see!

This person has **no** hair,
Work clothes are what they like to wear.
They like to watch **adverts** on TV,
And play **football** with me.
They like **cake** to eat,
And sometimes **cookies** for a treat.
Dancing is their favourite thing,
And **Twinkle, Twinkle Little Star** is what they sing.
Dylan is their best friend,
And now this riddle is at the end.

Have you guessed who it could be?
Look below and you will see, it is...

Answer: Uncle Mark.

Dylan French (4)

Inan's First Riddle

This is my riddle about an amazing animal.
What could it be?
Follow the clues to see!

This animal has **gills** on its body,
And its colour is **blue**.
This animal has **no** feet,
It likes **fish** to eat.
In the sea is where it lives,
Its favourite thing to do is **swim around and chase the fish**.
This animal has **two holes for** ears,
It makes **dun, dun, dun** sounds for you to hear.

Are you an animal whizz?
Have you guessed what it is?
It is...

Answer: A shark.

Inan Kaya (2)

Dubem's First Riddle

This is my riddle about a fantastic person.
Who could it be? Follow the clues to see!

This person has **brown** hair,
Braids are what they like to wear.
They like to watch **the news** on TV,
And play **snakes and ladders** with me.
They like **to give me food** to eat,
And sometimes **chocolate** for a treat.
Walking is their favourite thing,
And **God song** is what they sing.
Michelle is their best friend,
And now this riddle is at the end.

Have you guessed who it could be?
Look below and you will see, it is...

Answer: My mama.

Dubem Nwogbo (4)

Zahra's First Riddle

This is my riddle about a fantastic person.
Who could it be?
Follow the clues to see!

This person has **brown** hair,
Pink tops and leggings are what they like to wear.
They like to watch **Loud House** on TV,
And play **crafts** with me.
They like **cookies** to eat,
And sometimes **crisps** for a treat.
Playing **the violin** is their favourite thing,
And **Horrid Henry** is what they sing.
Dad is their best friend,
And now this riddle is at the end.

Have you guessed who it could be?
Look below and you will see, it is...

Answer: My mum.

Zahra Ben-Saïd (5)

Alberta's First Riddle

This is my riddle about a fantastic person.
Who could it be? Follow the clues to see!

This person has **white** hair,
Red is what they like to wear.
They like to watch **Christmas movies** on TV,
And play **snowball fights** with me.
They like **mince pies** to eat,
And sometimes **cookies** for a treat.
Making toys is their favourite thing,
And **Jingle Bells** is what they sing.
Everybody is their best friend,
And now this riddle is at the end.

Have you guessed who it could be?
Look below and you will see, it is...

Answer: Father Christmas.

Alberta London (4)

Lincoln's First Riddle

What could it be?
Follow the clues and see.

It looks **white and shiny**.
It sounds **noisy**.
It smells **like oil**.
It feels **hot and strong**.
It tastes **watery from raindrops**.

Have you guessed what it could be?
Look below and you will see,
It is...

Answer: A car.

Lincoln Graham (4)
Bangor Independent Christian School, Bangor

Betsy's First Riddle

What could it be?
Follow the clues and see.

It looks **like the sun**.
It sounds **crunchy**.
It smells **like spring**.
It feels **smooth**.
It tastes **like lemons**.

Have you guessed what it could be?
Look below and you will see,
It is...

Answer: A daffodil.

Betsy Jones (5)
Brynford County Primary School, Brynford

Elias' First Riddle

What could it be?
Follow the clues and see.

It looks **red and round**.
It sounds **like birds tweeting when they find it**.
It smells **sweet**.
It feels **smooth and squidgy**.
It tastes **sweet**.

Have you guessed what it could be?
Look below and you will see,
It is...

Answer: A berry.

Elias Baker (5)
Castle Park Primary School, Caldicot

Renaee's First Riddle

What could it be?
Follow the clues and see.

It looks **round**.
It sounds **like hooves**.
It smells **like milk**.
It feels **hairy**.
It tastes **like a Bounty**.

Have you guessed what it could be?
Look below and you will see,
It is...

Answer: A coconut.

Renaee Boulasi (4)
Castle Park Primary School, Caldicot

Esme's First Riddle

What could it be?
Follow the clues and see.

It looks **square**.
It sounds **squelchy**.
It smells **sweet and fruity**.
It feels **squishy**.
It tastes **delicious**.

Have you guessed what it could be?
Look below and you will see,
It is...

Answer: A chewy sweet.

Esme Harvey (5)
Castle Park Primary School, Caldicot

Gracie-May's First Riddle

What could it be?
Follow the clues and see.

It looks **like clouds**.
It sounds **all crunchy**.
It smells **so sweet**.
It feels **very rough**.
It tastes **so, so yummy**.

Have you guessed what it could be?
Look below and you will see,
It is...

Answer: Popcorn.

Gracie-May Bellamy (5)
Castle Park Primary School, Caldicot

Dylan's First Riddle

What could it be?
Follow the clues and see.

It looks **dark and scary**.
It sounds **crunchy, windy and rustly**.
It smells **fresh**.
It feels **muddy and soft**.
It tastes **earthy and leafy**.

Have you guessed what it could be?
Look below and you will see,
It is...

Answer: *The forest*.

Dylan Cook (5)
Corpus Christi Primary School, Glasgow

Wayne's First Riddle

What could it be?
Follow the clues and see.

It looks **yellow and blue**.
It sounds **like *squawk*!**
It smells **dusty**.
It feels **soft**.

Have you guessed what it could be?
Look below and you will see,
It is...

Answer: A macaw.

Wayne Rwizi (11)
Croftcroighn School, Glasgow

Charlie-Anne's First Riddle

What could it be?
Follow the clues and see.

It looks **grey and stripy**.
It sounds **like screaming**.
It feels **soft**.

Have you guessed what it could be?
Look below and you will see,
It is...

Answer: A lemur.

Charlie-Anne Bowes (10)
Croftcroighn School, Glasgow

Gabriel's First Riddle

What could it be?
Follow the clues and see.

It looks **big and stripy**.
It sounds **like *roar*!**
It feels **smooth**.

Have you guessed what it could be?
Look below and you will see,
It is...

Answer: *A tiger.*

Gabriel Eghobamien (11)
Croftcroighn School, Glasgow

James' First Riddle

What could it be?
Follow the clues and see.

It looks **black and brown and big.**
It sounds **like pigs grunting.**
It feels **furry.**

Have you guessed what it could be?
Look below and you will see,
It is...

Answer: A *gorilla*.

James Barnes (9)
Croftcroighn School, Glasgow

Lucas' First Riddle

What could it be?
Follow the clues and see.

It looks **green, yellow, red and small**.
It sounds **like buzzing**.
It feels **slimy**.

Have you guessed what it could be?
Look below and you will see,
It is...

Answer: A red-eyed tree frog.

Lucas McGinley (8)
Croftcroighn School, Glasgow

Darragh's First Riddle

What could it be?
Follow the clues and see.

It looks **big and feathery**.
It sounds **like *caw, caw, caw***.
It smells **wet and cold**.
It feels **soft and feathery**.
It tastes **like chicken**.

Have you guessed what it could be?
Look below and you will see,
It is...

Answer: An eagle.

Darragh Bradley (8)
Gaelscoil Éadain Mhóir, Brandywell

Cayden's First Riddle

What could it be?
Follow the clues and see.

It looks **spiky**.
It sounds **very quiet**.
It smells **bad**.
It feels **prickly**.
It tastes **awful**.

Have you guessed what it could be?
Look below and you will see,
It is...

Answer: A hedgehog.

Cayden Williams (8)
Gaelscoil Éadain Mhóir, Brandywell

Michael's First Riddle

What could it be?
Follow the clues and see.

It looks **wet**.
It sounds **quiet**.
It smells **disgusting**.
It feels **floppy and slimy**.
It tastes **nice**.

Have you guessed what it could be?
Look below and you will see,
It is...

Answer: A fish.

Michael Allen (7)
Gaelscoil Éadain Mhóir, Brandywell

Ruairí's First Riddle

What could it be?
Follow the clues and see.

It looks **small and scary**.
It sounds **quiet**.
It smells **bad**.
It feels **light**.
It tastes **poisonous**.

Have you guessed what it could be?
Look below and you will see,
It is...

Answer: A spider.

Ruairí Moore (7)
Gaelscoil Éadain Mhóir, Brandywell

Caislín's First Riddle

What could it be?
Follow the clues and see.

It looks **small and fluffy**.
It sounds **very loud**.
It smells **good or bad**.
It feels **soft and cuddly**.
It tastes **meaty**.

Have you guessed what it could be?
Look below and you will see,
It is...

Answer: A bunny.

Caislín Clarke (9)
Gaelscoil Éadain Mhóir, Brandywell

Killian's First Riddle

What could it be?
Follow the clues and see.

It looks **black and hairy**.
It sounds **quiet**.
It smells **like grass**.
It feels **soft and hairy**.
It tastes **like meat**.

Have you guessed what it could be?
Look below and you will see,
It is...

Answer: A tarantula.

Killian Harkin (8)
Gaelscoil Éadain Mhóir, Brandywell

Mia's First Riddle

What could it be?
Follow the clues and see.

It looks **white or brown and sometimes black.**
It sounds **loud.**
It smells **okay.**
It feels **very fluffy and soft.**
It tastes **meaty.**

Have you guessed what it could be?
Look below and you will see,
It is...

Answer: A rabbit.

Mia Pirone (8)
Gaelscoil Éadain Mhóir, Brandywell

Amber's First Riddle

What could it be?
Follow the clues and see.

It looks **colourful with snowy icing**.
It sounds **Christmassy**.
It smells **of ginger and sweeties**.
It feels **textured and hard**.
It tastes **yummy with Smarties and gummy bears**.

Have you guessed what it could be?
Look below and you will see,
It is...

Answer: A gingerbread house.

Amber Smithers (4)
Harleston CE Primary Academy, Harleston

Maxwell's First Riddle

What could it be?
Follow the clues and see.

It looks **yellow**.
It sounds **squelchy**.
It smells **yummy**.
It feels **slimy**.
It tastes **delicious**.

Have you guessed what it could be?
Look below and you will see,
It is...

Answer: Custard.

Maxwell Aldred
Harleston CE Primary Academy, Harleston

Archie's First Riddle

What could it be?
Follow the clues and see.

It looks **round and lumpy up high**.
It sounds **like a bell some say**.
It smells **like charcoal**.
It feels **rocky, dusty and sandy**.
It tastes **like cheese**.

Have you guessed what it could be?
Look below and you will see,
It is...

Answer: *The moon.*

Archie Cooper (5)
Harleston CE Primary Academy, Harleston

Ellie's First Riddle

What could it be?
Follow the clues and see.

It looks **oval**.
It sounds **like *crack***.
It smells **of stinky feet if it's bad**.
It feels **smooth in its shell**.
It tastes **yummy with toast**.

Have you guessed what it could be?
Look below and you will see,
It is...

Answer: An egg.

Ellie Robertson (6)
Killinchy Primary School, Killinchy

Zach's First Riddle

What could it be?
Follow the clues and see.

It looks **white**.
It sounds **splashy**.
It smells **milky**.
It feels **wet**.
It tastes **yummy**.

Have you guessed what it could be?
Look below and you will see,
It is...

Answer: Milk.

Zach Mitchell (5)
Killinchy Primary School, Killinchy

Noah's First Riddle

What could it be?
Follow the clues and see.

It looks **big**.
It sounds **noisy**.
It smells **oily**.
It feels **hard**.
It tastes **smoky**.

Have you guessed what it could be?
Look below and you will see,
It is...

Answer: A *steam train*.

Noah Caughey (5)
Killinchy Primary School, Killinchy

Erin's First Riddle

What could it be?
Follow the clues and see.

It looks **oval**.
It sounds **crunchy**.
It smells **sweet**.
It feels **rough**.
It tastes **yummy**.

Have you guessed what it could be?
Look below and you will see,
It is...

Answer: *Rice Krispies*.

Erin Shaw (4)
Killinchy Primary School, Killinchy

Freddy's First Riddle

What could it be?
Follow the clues and see.

It looks **smooth**.
It sounds **silent**.
It smells **sweet**.
It feels **cold**.
It tastes **yummy**.

Have you guessed what it could be?
Look below and you will see,
It is...

Answer: Vanilla ice cream.

Freddy Hunniford (5)
Killinchy Primary School, Killinchy

Rosa's First Riddle

What could it be?
Follow the clues and see.

It looks **beautiful**.
It sounds **quiet**.
It smells **like perfume**.
It feels **prickly**.
It tastes **yucky**.

Have you guessed what it could be?
Look below and you will see,
It is...

Answer: A rose.

Rosa Francis (5)
Killinchy Primary School, Killinchy

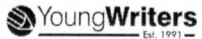

Will's First Riddle

What could it be?
Follow the clues and see.

It looks **like a circle**.
It sounds **happy**.
It smells **like chocolate**.
It feels **squishy**.
It tastes **yummy**.

Have you guessed what it could be?
Look below and you will see,
It is...

Answer: *Birthday cake.*

Will Agnew (5)
Killinchy Primary School, Killinchy

Daniel's First Riddle

What could it be?
Follow the clues and see.

It looks **orange and round**.
It sounds **hollow**.
It smells **sweet**.
It feels **smooth and hard**.
It tastes **good in a pie**.

Have you guessed what it could be?
Look below and you will see,
It is...

Answer: A pumpkin.

Daniel Gilmore (5)
Killinchy Primary School, Killinchy

Callum's First Riddle

What could it be?
Follow the clues and see.

It looks **like a small coconut**.
It sounds **like pee-wee**.
It smells **like cut grass**.
It feels **soft and furry**.
It tastes **sweet**.

Have you guessed what it could be?
Look below and you will see,
It is...

Answer: A kiwi.

Callum Wijkstra (5)
Killinchy Primary School, Killinchy

Maksis' First Riddle

What could it be?
Follow the clues and see.

It looks **like a rectangle**.
It sounds **like nothing**.
It smells **fresh**.
It feels **hard outside and soft inside**.
It tastes **chewy**.

Have you guessed what it could be?
Look below and you will see,
It is...

Answer: Chewing gum.

Maksis Briska-Emsins (5)
Killinchy Primary School, Killinchy

Molly's First Riddle

What could it be?
Follow the clues and see.

It looks **like worms**.
It sounds **like a click when it's dry**.
It smells **like pasta**.
It feels **slimy**.
It tastes **wet and yummy**.

Have you guessed what it could be?
Look below and you will see,
It is...

Answer: Spaghetti.

Molly Anderson (5)
Killinchy Primary School, Killinchy

Ollie's First Riddle

What could it be?
Follow the clues and see.

It looks **black and white or brown too**.
It sounds **like *moo***.
It smells **yuck**!
It feels **soft like fluff**.
It tastes **like grass and muck**.

Have you guessed what it could be?
Look below and you will see,
It is...

Answer: A cow.

Ollie Starbuck (5)
Killinchy Primary School, Killinchy

Eloise's First Riddle

What could it be?
Follow the clues and see.

It looks **a little brown and red**.
It sounds **crunchy and slurpy**.
It smells **yummy**.
It feels **spiky and warm**.
It tastes **tomatoey and buttery**.

Have you guessed what it could be?
Look below and you will see,
It is...

Answer: Beans on toast.

Eloise Reid (5)
Killinchy Primary School, Killinchy

Felix's First Riddle

This is my riddle about a fantastic person.
Who could it be? Follow the clues to see!

This person has **short, brown, straight** hair,
Blue silk shorts are what they like to wear.
They like to watch **Junior Bake Off** on TV,
And play **football** with me.
They like **delicious roast dinner** to eat,
And sometimes **smooth melting chocolate** for a treat.
Playing with me is their favourite thing,
And **pop songs** are what they sing.
Felix Nicholson is their best friend,
And now this riddle is at the end.

Have you guessed who it could be?
Look below and you will see, it is...

Answer: Max.

Felix Nicholson (4)
Manley Park Primary School, Whalley Range

Maya's First Riddle

This is my super first riddle.
What could it be?
Follow the clues to see!

The park is where you'll find it,
It's made out of **wood**.
It is used for **paper**,
Its colour is **brown**.
It is a **tall** shape,
It has **leaves**.

Have you guessed what it could be?
Look below and you will see,
It is...

Answer: A tree.

Maya Solomon-Thomas (5)
Manley Park Primary School, Whalley Range

Tabitha's First Riddle

This is my super first riddle.
What could it be?
Follow the clues to see!

In hair is where you'll find it,
It's made out of **plastic**.
It is used for **keeping hair back**,
Its colour is **yellow**.
It is a **butterfly** shape,
It has **glitter**.

Have you guessed what it could be?
Look below and you will see,
It is...

Answer: A clip.

Tabitha Percy (5)
Manley Park Primary School, Whalley Range

Sebastian's First Riddle

This is my super first riddle.
What could it be?
Follow the clues to see!

Underground is where you'll find it,
It's made out of **flesh and bones**.
It is used for **palaeontology**,
Its colour is **blue**.
It is a **big** shape,
It has **a tail**.

Have you guessed what it could be?
Look below and you will see,
It is...

Answer: A dinosaur.

Sebastian Alton (5)
Manley Park Primary School, Whalley Range

Benji's First Riddle

This is my super first riddle.
What could it be?
Follow the clues to see!

In the kitchen is where you'll find it,
It's made out of **hard clay**.
It is used for **food**,
Its colour is **dark blue**.
It is a **circle** shape,
It has **a spoon so you can eat**.

Have you guessed what it could be?
Look below and you will see,
It is...

Answer: A bowl.

Benjamin McHague (4)
Manley Park Primary School, Whalley Range

Agnes' First Riddle

This is my super first riddle.
What could it be?
Follow the clues to see!

In a toy basket is where you'll find it,
It's made out of **fluff**.
It is used for **playing**,
Its colour is **dark purple**.
It is a **soft toy** shape,
It has **ears and claws**.

Have you guessed what it could be?
Look below and you will see,
It is...

Answer: A toy teddy bear.

Agnes Oliveira (5)
Manley Park Primary School, Whalley Range

Theo's First Riddle

This is my riddle about a brilliant vehicle.
What could it be?
Follow the clues to see!

It has **two** wheels,
Fast is the speed it goes.
Its colour is **bright yellow**,
Only one person can fit in it,
The engine is how it moves,
People use it to go to **mostly everywhere**.

Have you guessed what it could be?
Look below and you will see,
It is...

Answer: A motorbike.

Theo Nolan (5)
Manley Park Primary School, Whalley Range

Sylvia's First Riddle

This is my riddle about an amazing animal.
What could it be?
Follow the clues to see!

This animal has **a fluffy tail** on its body,
And its colour is **white**.
This animal has **special jumping** feet,
It likes **carrots** to eat.
Burrow is where it lives,
Its favourite thing to do is **hop**.
This animal has **long** ears,
It makes **a nibbly** sound for you to hear.

Are you an animal whizz?
Have you guessed what it is?
It is...

Answer: A bunny.

Sylvia Marshall (5)
Manley Park Primary School, Whalley Range

Aoife's First Riddle

This is my riddle about an amazing animal.
What could it be?
Follow the clues to see!

This animal has **big teeth** on its body,
And its colour is **yellow**.
This animal has **four little** feet,
It likes **animals** to eat.
In a cave is where it lives,
Its favourite thing to do is **sleep**.
This animal has **big, soft** ears,
It makes **loud roar** sounds for you to hear.

Are you an animal whizz?
Have you guessed what it is?
It is...

Answer: A lion.

Aoife Hodkinson (5)
Manley Park Primary School, Whalley Range

Daisy's First Riddle

This is my riddle about an amazing animal.
What could it be?
Follow the clues to see!

This animal has **stripes** on its body,
And its colours are **orange and black**.
This animal has **stompy** feet,
It likes **grass** to eat.
The jungle is where it lives,
Its favourite thing to do is **eat grass**.
This animal has **big** ears,
It makes **scary roar** sounds for you to hear.

Are you an animal whizz?
Have you guessed what it is?
It is…

Answer: A tiger.

Daisy Wild (4)
Manley Park Primary School, Whalley Range

Zainab's First Riddle

This is my riddle about an amazing animal.
What could it be?
Follow the clues to see!

This animal has **a long tail** on its body,
And its colour is **light ginger**.
This animal has **four little** feet,
It likes **sparkly fish** to eat.
In a little house is where it lives,
Its favourite thing to do is **catch mice**.
This animal has **pointy** ears,
It makes **purring** sounds for you to hear.

Are you an animal whizz?
Have you guessed what it is?
It is...

Answer: A cat.

Zainab Zafar (5)
Manley Park Primary School, Whalley Range

Silvie's First Riddle

This is my riddle about an amazing animal.
What could it be?
Follow the clues to see!

This animal has **green, slimy skin** on its body,
And its colour is **light green.**
This animal has **slimy, green, bouncy** feet,
It likes **small flies** to eat.
In a pond and on a lily is where it lives,
Its favourite thing to do is **jump on lily pads.**
This animal has **slimy, teeny** ears,
It makes **ribbit, ribbit** sounds for you to hear.

Are you an animal whizz?
Have you guessed what it is?
It is...

Answer: A frog.

Silvie Naidu (5)
Manley Park Primary School, Whalley Range

Rubi's First Riddle

This is my riddle about a fantastic person.
Who could it be? Follow the clues to see!

This person has **bright red** hair,
Glasses are what they like to wear.
They like to watch **crime drama** on TV,
And play **hide-and-seek** with me.
They like **fruit** to eat,
And sometimes **jam cake** for a treat.
Cutting is their favourite thing,
And **Miss Polly Had A Dolly** is what they sing.
Miss McDonugh is their best friend,
And now this riddle is at the end.

Have you guessed who it could be?
Look below and you will see, it is...

Answer: Miss Skelton.

Rubi Alam (5)
Manley Park Primary School, Whalley Range

William's First Riddle

This is my riddle about a fantastic person.
Who could it be? Follow the clues to see!

This person has **smooth blonde** hair,
Blue jeans are what they like to wear.
They like to watch **baking programmes** on TV,
And play **racing cars** with me.
They like **crispy duck** to eat,
And sometimes **ice cream** for a treat.
Resting is their favourite thing,
And **nursery rhymes** are what they sing.
Gerard is their best friend,
And now this riddle is at the end.

Have you guessed who it could be?
Look below and you will see, it is...

Answer: My daddy.

William Stone (5)
Manley Park Primary School, Whalley Range

Jordi's First Riddle

What could it be?
Follow the clues and see.

It looks **like it's night-time but the sun is still out**.
It sounds **angry and scary but it's the smallest in the family.**
It smells **of jungle bark and leaves and fruit.**
It feels **warm and cuddly.**
It tastes **sweet, sticky honey with a very long tongue.**

Have you guessed what it could be?
Look below and you will see,
It is...

Answer: A sun bear.

Jordi Marks (5)
Mullaglass Primary School, Newry

Clara's First Riddle

What could it be?
Follow the clues and see.

It looks **like a tree**.
It sounds **crunchy**.
It smells **earthy**.
It feels **bumpy**.
It tastes **sweet**.

Have you guessed what it could be?
Look below and you will see,
It is...

Answer: Broccoli.

Clara Jones (5)
Mullaglass Primary School, Newry

Callum's First Riddle

What could it be?
Follow the clues and see.

It looks **big and white**.
It sounds **loud and scary**.
It smells **of fish**.
It feels **cold and hairy**.
It tastes **like steak**.

Have you guessed what it could be?
Look below and you will see,
It is...

Answer: A polar bear.

Callum Marshall (5)
Mullaglass Primary School, Newry

Cory's First Riddle

What could it be?
Follow the clues and see.

It looks **round and tubby**.
It sounds **like it has a cold**.
It smells **like outdoors**.
It feels **fluffy**.
It tastes **like honey**.

Have you guessed what it could be?
Look below and you will see,
It is...

Answer: *Winnie the Pooh*.

Cory Yates (5)
Mullaglass Primary School, Newry

Oliver First Riddle

What could it be?
Follow the clues and see.

It looks **snuggly and scary.**
It sounds **as quiet as the snow.**
It smells **of fish and seals.**
It feels **soft and cuddly.**
It tastes **yucky.**

Have you guessed what it could be?
Look below and you will see,
It is...

Answer: A polar bear.

Oliver Patterson (5)
Mullaglass Primary School, Newry

Emily's First Riddle

What could it be?
Follow the clues and see.

It looks **like a big teddy bear.**
It sounds **dangerous when it growls.**
It smells **like snowflakes.**
It feels **soft when you stroke it.**
It tastes **like Milky buttons.**

Have you guessed what it could be?
Look below and you will see,
It is...

Answer: A polar bear.

Emily Moffett (5)
Mullaglass Primary School, Newry

Jack's First Riddle

What could it be?
Follow the clues and see.

It looks **black and white**.
It sounds **crunchy when it's stomping on bamboo**.
It smells **bad when it's wet**.
It feels **soft and cuddly**.
It tastes **crunchy bamboo leaves**.

Have you guessed what it could be?
Look below and you will see,
It is...

Answer: A panda.

Jack Laverty (5)
Mullaglass Primary School, Newry

Jessica First Riddle

Who could it be?
Follow the clues and see.

He looks **cute with his blue coat and red hat.**
He sounds **scared and lonely.**
He smells **lovely and tasty like marmalade.**
He feels **soft and so cuddly.**
He tastes **marmalade sandwiches.**

Have you guessed who it could be?
Look below and you will see,
It is...

Answer: Paddington Bear.

Jessica Copeland (6)
Mullaglass Primary School, Newry

Poppy's First Riddle

What could it be?
Follow the clues and see.

It looks **like I have rubbed coal on my eyes**.
It sounds **quiet as we are endangered**.
It smells **woody and mountain fresh**.
It feels **soft and woolly like a teddy**.
It tastes **like bamboo and leaves**.

Have you guessed what it could be?
Look below and you will see,
It is...

Answer: A panda bear.

Poppy Baird (4)
Mullaglass Primary School, Newry

Olivia's First Riddle

This is my riddle about an amazing animal.
What could it be?
Follow the clues to see!

This animal has **feathers** on its body,
And its colours are **like a rainbow**.
This animal has **claws on its** feet,
It likes **seeds and fruit** to eat.
Rainforests are where it lives,
Its favourite thing to do is **copying what you say**.
This animal has **secret** ears,
It makes **loud squawky** sounds for you to hear.

Are you an animal whizz?
Have you guessed what it is?
It is...

Answer: A parrot.

Olivia Boyden (5)
Oakdale Primary School, Stanground

Harry's First Riddle

What could it be?
Follow the clues and see.

It looks **colourful and pretty**.
It sounds **as quiet as a mouse**.
It smells **of the air**.
It feels **soft and smooth**.
It tastes **the leaves on the bushes**.

Have you guessed what it could be?
Look below and you will see,
It is...

Answer: A butterfly.

Harry Forth (5)
Oakdale Primary School, Stanground

Jacob's First Riddle

This is my super first riddle.
What could it be?
Follow the clues to see!

Deep, dark space is where you'll find it,
It's made out of **metal**.
It is used for **taking pictures**,
Its colours are **orange, black, white and a bit of grey**.
It is a **circle** shape,
It has **three booms with special equipment**.

Have you guessed what it could be?
Look below and you will see,
It is...

Answer: *Voyager 1*.

Jacob Silva-Banks (5)
Oakdale Primary School, Stanground

Ashley's First Riddle

What could it be?
Follow the clues and see.

It looks **like a little ball of fuzz.**
It sounds **like a loud humming buzz.**
It smells **flowers with its tiny nose.**
It feels **heavy when wet by a hose.**
It tastes **the nectar and makes honey so sweet, it flies to the hive with pollen on its feet.**

Have you guessed what it could be?
Look below and you will see,
It is...

Answer: A bee.

Ashley Brighton (5)
Oakdale Primary School, Stanground

Adam's First Riddle

What could it be?
Follow the clues and see.

It looks **pretty**.
It sounds **beautiful**.
It smells **like love**.
It feels **soft**.
It tastes **like jelly**.

Have you guessed what it could be?
Look below and you will see,
It is...

Answer: A rose.

Adam Stajuda (4)
Penybont Primary School, Bridgend

Ethan's First Riddle

What could it be?
Follow the clues and see.

It looks **red**.
It sounds **silent**.
It smells **sweet**.
It feels **soft**.
It tastes **nice**.

Have you guessed what it could be?
Look below and you will see,
It is...

Answer: A rose.

Ethan Mason (5)
Penybont Primary School, Bridgend

Morgan's First Riddle

What could it be?
Follow the clues and see.

It looks **lovely**.
It sounds **quiet**.
It smells **lush**.
It feels **soft**.
It tastes **cold**.

Have you guessed what it could be?
Look below and you will see,
It is...

Answer: A rose.

Morgan Schokkenbroek (4)
Penybont Primary School, Bridgend

Jasmine's First Riddle

What could it be?
Follow the clues and see.

It looks **round**.
It sounds **heavy**.
It smells **nice**.
It feels **smooth**.
It tastes **yummy**.

Have you guessed what it could be?
Look below and you will see,
It is...

Answer: Mango.

Jasmine McLennon (5)
Penybont Primary School, Bridgend

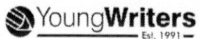

Leia's First Riddle

What could it be?
Follow the clues and see.

It looks **red**.
It sounds **like a kiss**.
It smells **lovely**.
It feels **soft**.
It tastes **lush**.

Have you guessed what it could be?
Look below and you will see,
It is...

Answer: A rose.

Leia Jury (4)
Penybont Primary School, Bridgend

Reuben's First Riddle

What could it be?
Follow the clues and see.

It looks **red**.
It sounds **quiet**.
It smells **flowery**.
It feels **like skin**.
It tastes **yucky**.

Have you guessed what it could be?
Look below and you will see,
It is...

Answer: A rose.

Reuben Hughes (5)
Penybont Primary School, Bridgend

Esme's First Riddle

What could it be?
Follow the clues and see.

It looks **green**.
It sounds **heavy**.
It smells **greasy**.
It feels **smooth**.
It tastes **juicy**.

Have you guessed what it could be?
Look below and you will see,
It is...

Answer: Watermelon.

Esme Colwill Downs (5)
Penybont Primary School, Bridgend

Joe's First Riddle

What could it be?
Follow the clues and see.

It looks **big**.
It sounds **of nothing**.
It smells **sweet**.
It feels **spiky**.
It tastes **yummy**.

Have you guessed what it could be?
Look below and you will see,
It is...

Answer: A pineapple.

Joe Beckinsale (5)
Penybont Primary School, Bridgend

Rex's First Riddle

What could it be?
Follow the clues and see.

It looks **like a sphere**.
It sounds **heavy**.
It smells **nice**.
It feels **smooth**.
It tastes **nice**.

Have you guessed what it could be?
Look below and you will see,
It is...

Answer: Watermelon.

Rex Carp (5)
Penybont Primary School, Bridgend

Charlie's First Riddle

What could it be?
Follow the clues and see.

It looks **beautiful**.
It sounds **like a whisper**.
It smells **lovely**.
It feels **nice**.
It tastes **like breakfast**.

Have you guessed what it could be?
Look below and you will see,
It is...

Answer: A rose.

Charlie Tunster-Price (5)
Penybont Primary School, Bridgend

Reubin's First Riddle

What could it be?
Follow the clues and see.

It looks **like a sphere**.
It sounds **heavy**.
It smells **nice**.
It feels **hard**.
It tastes **yummy**.

Have you guessed what it could be?
Look below and you will see,
It is...

Answer: *Pomegranate*.

Reubin Fletcher (5)
Penybont Primary School, Bridgend

Clara's First Riddle

What could it be?
Follow the clues and see.

It looks **pointy at the bottom**.
It sounds **crunchy**.
It smells **like soil**.
It feels **hard**.
It tastes **nice cooked**.

Have you guessed what it could be?
Look below and you will see,
It is...

Answer: A carrot.

Clara Eddies (4)
Perry Hall Primary School, Wednesfield

Ryley's First Riddle

What could it be?
Follow the clues and see.

It looks **brown**.
It sounds **crunchy**.
It feels **warm**.
It tastes **spicy**.

Have you guessed what it could be?
Look below and you will see,
It is...

Answer: An onion.

Ryley Redford
Perry Hall Primary School, Wednesfield

William's First Riddle

What could it be?
Follow the clues and see.

It looks **round**.
It sounds **crunchy**.
It smells **sweet**.
It tastes **yucky**.

Have you guessed what it could be?
Look below and you will see,
It is...

Answer: An onion.

William Wilkinson (5)
Perry Hall Primary School, Wednesfield

Japji's First Riddle

What could it be?
Follow the clues and see.

It looks **red**.
It sounds **crunchy**.
It smells **good**.
It feels **cold**.
It tastes **nice**.

Have you guessed what it could be?
Look below and you will see,
It is...

Answer: An apple.

Japji Shergill (5)
Perry Hall Primary School, Wednesfield

Lyla's First Riddle

What could it be?
Follow the clues and see.

It looks **round**.
It sounds **crunchy**.
It smells **wet**.
It feels **soft**.
It tastes **sweet**.

Have you guessed what it could be?
Look below and you will see,
It is...

Answer: An apple.

Lyla Gardner (5)
Perry Hall Primary School, Wednesfield

Holly's First Riddle

What could it be?
Follow the clues and see.

It looks **green**.
It sounds **chewy**.
It smells **sweet**.
It feels **cold**.
It tastes **juicy**.

Have you guessed what it could be?
Look below and you will see,
It is...

Answer: An apple.

Holly Tanner (4)
Perry Hall Primary School, Wednesfield

Travis' First Riddle

What could it be?
Follow the clues and see.

It looks **round**.
It sounds **crunchy**.
It smells **bad**.
It feels **hard**.
It tastes **spicy**.

Have you guessed what it could be?
Look below and you will see,
It is...

Answer: An onion.

Travis Scordis-Hutchinson (5)
Perry Hall Primary School, Wednesfield

Sebastian's First Riddle

What could it be?
Follow the clues and see.

It looks **red**.
It sounds **crunchy**.
It smells **yummy**.
It feels **hard**.
It tastes **juicy**.

Have you guessed what it could be?
Look below and you will see,
It is...

Answer: An apple.

Sebastian Smith (4)
Perry Hall Primary School, Wednesfield

Muhammad's First Riddle

What could it be?
Follow the clues and see.

It looks **yellow**.
It sounds **noisy**.
It smells **sweet**.
It feels **hard**.
It tastes **juicy**.

Have you guessed what it could be?
Look below and you will see,
It is...

Answer: A lemon.

Muhammad Masab (5)
Perry Hall Primary School, Wednesfield

Avneet's First Riddle

What could it be?
Follow the clues and see.

It looks **long**.
It sounds **crunchy**.
It smells **oily**.
It feels **cold**.
It tastes **yummy**.

Have you guessed what it could be?
Look below and you will see,
It is...

Answer: A carrot.

Avneet Ghakal (5)
Perry Hall Primary School, Wednesfield

Jasleen's First Riddle

What could it be?
Follow the clues and see.

It looks **yellow**.
It sounds **noisy**.
It smells **sweet**.
It feels **soft**.
It tastes **good**.

Have you guessed what it could be?
Look below and you will see,
It is...

Answer: A pepper.

Jasleen Kahlon (4)
Perry Hall Primary School, Wednesfield

Harley's First Riddle

What could it be?
Follow the clues and see.

It looks **round**.
It sounds **crunchy**.
It smells **sweet**.
It feels **cold**.
It tastes **yummy**.

Have you guessed what it could be?
Look below and you will see,
It is...

Answer: An apple.

Harley Thomas (5)
Perry Hall Primary School, Wednesfield

Roop's First Riddle

What could it be?
Follow the clues and see.

It looks **yellow**.
It sounds **crunchy**.
It smells **sour**.
It feels **hard**.
It tastes **spicy**.

Have you guessed what it could be?
Look below and you will see,
It is...

Answer: A pepper.

Roop Sandhu (5)
Perry Hall Primary School, Wednesfield

Joshua's First Riddle

What could it be?
Follow the clues and see.

It looks **yellow**.
It sounds **juicy**.
It smells **nice**.
It feels **hard**.
It tastes **horrible**.

Have you guessed what it could be?
Look below and you will see,
It is...

Answer: A lemon.

Joshua Arrowsmith (4)
Perry Hall Primary School, Wednesfield

Mason's First Riddle

What could it be?
Follow the clues and see.

It looks **yellow**.
It sounds **juicy**.
It smells **juicy**.
It feels **squishy**.
It tastes **sweet**.

Have you guessed what it could be?
Look below and you will see,
It is...

Answer: A lemon.

Mason Humpage (4)
Perry Hall Primary School, Wednesfield

Amara's First Riddle

What could it be?
Follow the clues and see.

It looks **round**.
It sounds **crunchy**.
It smells **sweet**.
It feels **smooth**.
It tastes **sweet**.

Have you guessed what it could be?
Look below and you will see,
It is...

Answer: An apple.

Amara Summan (5)
Perry Hall Primary School, Wednesfield

Seth's First Riddle

What could it be?
Follow the clues and see.

It looks **pointy**.
It sounds **crunchy**.
It smells **yucky**.
It feels **smooth**.
It tastes **spicy**.

Have you guessed what it could be?
Look below and you will see,
It is...

Answer: A pepper.

Seth Brown (5)
Perry Hall Primary School, Wednesfield

Archie's First Riddle

What could it be?
Follow the clues and see.

It looks **pointy**.
It sounds **crunchy**.
It smells **weird**.
It feels **smooth**.
It tastes **strong**.

Have you guessed what it could be?
Look below and you will see,
It is...

Answer: A pepper.

Archie Marshall (4)
Perry Hall Primary School, Wednesfield

Demi-Leigh's First Riddle

What could it be?
Follow the clues and see.

It looks **long**.
It sounds **crunchy**.
It smells **like soil**.
It feels **bumpy**.
It tastes **sweet**.

Have you guessed what it could be?
Look below and you will see,
It is...

Answer: A carrot.

Demi-Leigh Davies (6)
Perry Hall Primary School, Wednesfield

Nishaan's First Riddle

What could it be?
Follow the clues and see.

It looks **red**.
It sounds **crunchy**.
It smells **like a flower**.
It feels **hard**.
It tastes **good**.

Have you guessed what it could be?
Look below and you will see,
It is...

Answer: An apple.

Nishaan Kooner (5)
Perry Hall Primary School, Wednesfield

Aliyah's First Riddle

What could it be?
Follow the clues and see.

It looks **round**.
It sounds **crunchy**.
It smells **strong**.
It feels **crunchy**.
It tastes **strong**.

Have you guessed what it could be?
Look below and you will see,
It is...

Answer: An onion.

Aliyah Summan (5)
Perry Hall Primary School, Wednesfield

Sophia's First Riddle

What could it be?
Follow the clues and see.

It looks **round**.
It sounds **crunchy**.
It smells **like nothing**.
It feels **cold**.
It tastes **sweet**.

Have you guessed what it could be?
Look below and you will see,
It is...

Answer: An apple.

Sophia Hazell (5)
Perry Hall Primary School, Wednesfield

Logan's First Riddle

What could it be?
Follow the clues and see.

It looks **like a circle**.
It sounds **crunchy**.
It smells **sweet**.
It feels **hard**.
It tastes **good**.

Have you guessed what it could be?
Look below and you will see,
It is...

Answer: *An apple.*

Logan Cooper (5)
Perry Hall Primary School, Wednesfield

Tyler's First Riddle

What could it be?
Follow the clues and see.

It looks **yellow**.
It sounds **stinky**.
It smells **like flowers**.
It feels **sticky**.
It tastes **spicy**.

Have you guessed what it could be?
Look below and you will see,
It is...

Answer: A lemon.

Tyler Farnell (4)
Perry Hall Primary School, Wednesfield

Ekam's First Riddle

What could it be?
Follow the clues and see.

It looks **round and brown**.
It sounds **crunchy**.
It smells **spicy**.
It feels **hard**.
It tastes **yuck**.

Have you guessed what it could be?
Look below and you will see,
It is...

Answer: An onion.

Ekam Sekhon (5)
Perry Hall Primary School, Wednesfield

Hollie's First Riddle

What could it be?
Follow the clues and see.

It looks **long**.
It sounds **crunchy**.
It smells **sweet**.
It feels **smooth and bumpy**.
It tastes **sweet**.

Have you guessed what it could be?
Look below and you will see,
It is...

Answer: A carrot.

Hollie Webster (5)
Perry Hall Primary School, Wednesfield

Anayah's First Riddle

What could it be?
Follow the clues and see.

It looks **like a snowman**.
It sounds **crunchy**.
It smells **like soil**.
It feels **bumpy**.
It tastes **sweet**.

Have you guessed what it could be?
Look below and you will see,
It is...

Answer: A carrot.

Anayah Cadot (4)
Perry Hall Primary School, Wednesfield

Jenso's First Riddle

What could it be?
Follow the clues and see.

It looks **green**.
It sounds **crunchy**.
It smells **like an apple**.
It feels **hard**.
It tastes **like water**.

Have you guessed what it could be?
Look below and you will see,
It is...

Answer: A cucumber.

Jenson Rogers (4)
Perry Hall Primary School, Wednesfield

Emilia's First Riddle

What could it be?
Follow the clues and see.

It looks **orange and bent**.
It sounds **crunchy**.
It smells **spicy**.
It feels **soft and smooth**.
It tastes **delicious**.

Have you guessed what it could be?
Look below and you will see,
It is...

Answer: A pepper.

Emilia Smith (5)
Perry Hall Primary School, Wednesfield

Evan's First Riddle

What could it be?
Follow the clues and see.

It looks **like clay**.
It sounds **crunchy**.
It smells **strong**.
It feels **smooth**.
It tastes **strong**.

Have you guessed what it could be?
Look below and you will see,
It is...

Answer: A pepper.

Evan Andrews (4)
Perry Hall Primary School, Wednesfield

Mia's First Riddle

This is my riddle about an amazing animal.
What could it be?
Follow the clues to see!

This animal has **short, soft fur** on its body,
And its colour is **brown.**
This animal has **four hooves for** feet,
It likes **sweet hay** to eat.
In the field is where it lives,
Its favourite thing to do is **eat crunchy carrots.**
This animal has **long, smooth** ears,
It makes **'heehaw'** sounds for you to hear.

Are you an animal whizz?
Have you guessed what it is?
It is...

Answer: A donkey.

Mia Vatunitu (4)
St Fagans CW Primary School, Michaelston Super Ely

Darren's First Riddle

This is my riddle about an amazing animal.
What could it be?
Follow the clues to see!

This animal has **a tail** on its body,
And its colour is **brown**.
This animal has **four** feet,
It likes **dog food** to eat.

Are you an animal whizz?
Have you guessed what it is?
It is…

Answer: A dog.

Darren Martinson (4)
St Fagans CW Primary School, Michaelston Super Ely

Phoebe's First Riddle

This is my riddle about an amazing animal.
What could it be?
Follow the clues to see!

This animal has **fluff** on its body,
And its colour is **brown**.
This animal has **small** feet,
It likes **meat** to eat.
My house is where it lives,
Its favourite thing to do is **sleep**.
This animal has **pointy** ears,
It makes **woofing** sounds for you to hear.

Are you an animal whizz?
Have you guessed what it is?
It is...

Answer: A dog.

Phoebe Roberts (5)
St Fagans CW Primary School, Michaelston Super Ely

Elliott's First Riddle

This is my riddle about an amazing animal.
What could it be?
Follow the clues to see!

This animal has **tough skin** on its body,
And its colour is **white and grey**.
This animal has **no** feet,
It likes **fish** to eat.
In the sea is where it lives,
Its favourite thing to do is **swim**.
This animal has **no** ears,
It makes **no** sounds for you to hear.

Are you an animal whizz?
Have you guessed what it is?
It is...

Answer: A shark.

Elliott Davey (4)
St Fagans CW Primary School, Michaelston Super Ely

Ellis' First Riddle

This is my riddle about an amazing animal.
What could it be?
Follow the clues to see!

This animal has **fur** on its body,
And its colour is **orange and black**.
This animal has **four** feet,
It likes **meat** to eat.
In the forest is where it lives,
Its favourite thing to do is **run**.
This animal has **furry** ears,
It makes **roaring** sounds for you to hear.

Are you an animal whizz?
Have you guessed what it is?
It is...

Answer: A tiger.

Ellis Dodd (5)
St Fagans CW Primary School, Michaelston Super Ely

Willow's First Riddle

This is my riddle about an amazing animal.
What could it be?
Follow the clues to see!

This animal has **fluffy fur** on its body,
And its colour is **white**.
This animal has **little** feet,
It likes **carrots** to eat.
In a cave is where it lives,
Its favourite thing to do is **hop**.
This animal has **long, fluffy** ears,
It makes **bunny** sounds for you to hear.

Are you an animal whizz?
Have you guessed what it is?
It is...

Answer: A bunny.

Willow Reddin (5)
St Fagans CW Primary School, Michaelston Super Ely

Elsie's First Riddle

This is my riddle about an amazing animal.
What could it be?
Follow the clues to see!

This animal is **fluffy** on its body,
And its colour is **brown and white.**
This animal has **white, short** feet,
It likes **bones** to eat.
A cosy bed is where it lives,
Its favourite thing to do is **play.**
This animal has **short** ears,
It makes **woofing** sounds for you to hear.

Are you an animal whizz?
Have you guessed what it is?
It is...

Answer: A dog.

Elsie Rhoden (5)
St Fagans CW Primary School, Michaelston Super Ely

Sebastian's First Riddle

This is my riddle about an amazing animal.
What could it be?
Follow the clues to see!

This animal has **stripes** on its body,
And its colour is **orange and black.**
This animal has **four** feet,
It likes **meat** to eat.
In the jungle is where it lives,
Its favourite thing to do is **roar.**
This animal has **pointy** ears,
It makes **roaring** sounds for you to hear.

Are you an animal whizz?
Have you guessed what it is?
It is...

Answer: A tiger.

Sebastian Child (4)
St Fagans CW Primary School, Michaelston Super Ely

Maddison's First Riddle

This is my riddle about an amazing animal.
What could it be?
Follow the clues to see!

This animal has **spotty fur** on its body,
And its colour is **yellow and black.**
This animal has **paws, not** feet,
It likes **yummy meat** to eat.
In a jungle is where it lives,
Its favourite thing to do is **playing.**
This animal has **little** ears,
It makes **growling** sounds for you to hear.

Are you an animal whizz?
Have you guessed what it is?
It is...

Answer: A leopard.

Maddison Slack (5)
St Fagans CW Primary School, Michaelston Super Ely

Mollie's First Riddle

This is my riddle about an amazing animal.
What could it be?
Follow the clues to see!

This animal has **black, soft fur** on its body,
And its colour is **bright blue**.
This animal has **no** feet,
It likes **sweet nectar** to eat.
On the flowers is where it lives,
Its favourite thing to do is **fly about**.
This animal has **no** ears,
It makes **fluttering** sounds for you to hear.

Are you an animal whizz?
Have you guessed what it is?
It is...

Answer: A butterfly.

Mollie Waters (4)
St Fagans CW Primary School, Michaelston Super Ely

Freya-L'ren's First Riddle

This is my riddle about an amazing animal.
What could it be?
Follow the clues to see!

This animal has **a sparkly shell** on its body,
And its colour is **yellow and brown.**
This animal has **fat and short** feet,
It likes **tasty lettuce** to eat.
A leafy garden is where it lives,
Its favourite thing to do is **eat grass**.
This animal has **tiny** ears,
It makes **grunting** sounds for you to hear.

Are you an animal whizz?
Have you guessed what it is?
It is...

Answer: A tortoise.

Freya-L'ren Smith (5)
St Fagans CW Primary School, Michaelston Super Ely

Lola's First Riddle

This is my riddle about an amazing animal.
What could it be?
Follow the clues to see!

This animal has **soft fur** on its body,
And its colour is **yellow, big**.
This animal has **big** feet,
It likes **other animals** to eat.
In a cave is where it lives,
Its favourite thing to do is **sleep
on the rocks**.
This animal has **little** ears,
It makes **roaring** sounds for you to hear.

Are you an animal whizz?
Have you guessed what it is?
It is...

Answer: A lion.

Lola (5)
St Fagans CW Primary School, Michaelston Super Ely

154

Harry's First Riddle

This is my riddle about an amazing animal.
What could it be?
Follow the clues to see!

This animal has **shiny fur** on its body,
And its colour is **yellow**.
This animal has **big, strong** feet,
It likes **meat** to eat.
On the rocks is where it lives,
Its favourite thing to do is **sleep on the rocks**.
This animal has **little, round** ears,
It makes **roaring** sounds for you to hear.

Are you an animal whizz?
Have you guessed what it is?
It is...

Answer: A lion.

Harry Winch (5)
St Fagans CW Primary School, Michaelston Super Ely

Zara's First Riddle

This is my riddle about an amazing animal.
What could it be?
Follow the clues to see!

This animal has **colourful stripes** on its body,
And its colour is **orange and white**.
This animal has **no** feet,
It likes **plants and worms** to eat.
The dark water is where it lives,
Its favourite thing to do is **swim in the coral reef**.
This animal has **no** ears,
It makes **air popping** sounds for you to hear.

Are you an animal whizz?
Have you guessed what it is?
It is...

Answer: A clownfish.

Zara Gafuri (5)
St Fagans CW Primary School, Michaelston Super Ely

Indigo's First Riddle

This is my riddle about an amazing animal.
What could it be?
Follow the clues to see!

This animal has **beautifully coloured wings** on its body,
And its colour is **sparkly red and blue**.
This animal has **no** feet,
It likes **nectar** to eat.
In flowers is where it lives,
Its favourite thing to do is **collect nectar**.
This animal has **antennae for** ears,
It makes **fluttering** sounds for you to hear.

Are you an animal whizz?
Have you guessed what it is?
It is...

Answer: A **butterfly**.

Indigo Grant (4)
St Fagans CW Primary School, Michaelston Super Ely

Antonina's First Riddle

What could it be?
Follow the clues and see.

It looks **pointy with round bits**.
It sounds **like crackly ice**.
It smells **like strawberry**.
It feels **cold and smooth**.
It tastes **like yummy vanilla**.

Have you guessed what it could be?
Look below and you will see,
It is...

Answer: Ice cream.

Antonina Krasuska (5)
St Mungo's Primary School & Nursery Class, Glasgow

Kye's First Riddle

What could it be?
Follow the clues and see.

It looks **yummy**.
It sounds **hard**.
It smells **good**.
It feels **hard**.
It tastes **delicious**.

Have you guessed what it could be?
Look below and you will see,
It is...

Answer: Chocolate.

Kye Chigwada (5)
St Mungo's Primary School & Nursery Class, Glasgow

Abdulaziz's First Riddle

What could it be?
Follow the clues and see.

It looks **yummy**.
It sounds **juicy**.
It smells **orangey**.
It feels **round and smooth**.
It tastes **yummy**.

Have you guessed what it could be?
Look below and you will see,
It is...

Answer: An orange.

Abdulaziz Othman (5)
St Mungo's Primary School & Nursery Class, Glasgow

Sarah's First Riddle

What could it be?
Follow the clues and see.

It looks **like a raindrop**.
It sounds **soft**.
It smells **nice and sweet**.
It feels **banging**.
It tastes **nice**.

Have you guessed what it could be?
Look below and you will see,
It is...

Answer: A pear.

Sarah Angela Reid (6)
St Mungo's Primary School & Nursery Class, Glasgow

Maria's First Riddle

What could it be?
Follow the clues and see.

It looks **soft and fluffy**.
It sounds **very quiet**.
It smells **of nothing**.
It feels **soft and squishy**.
It tastes **of nothing**.

Have you guessed what it could be?
Look below and you will see,
It is...

Answer: A teddy bear.

Maria Alexandra Vargas Teixeira (5)
St Mungo's Primary School & Nursery Class, Glasgow

Cooper's First Riddle

What could it be?
Follow the clues and see.

It looks **good**.
It sounds **delicious**.
It smells **sweet and tasty**.
It feels **cold and slippery**.
It tastes **like bubblegum**.

Have you guessed what it could be?
Look below and you will see,
It is...

Answer: Ice cream.

Cooper Mullan (6)
St Mungo's Primary School & Nursery Class, Glasgow

Lewis' First Riddle

What could it be?
Follow the clues and see.

It looks **like robots and Minecraft.**
It sounds **like rain and noise.**
It smells **of nothing.**
It feels **like the beach.**
It tastes **of nothing.**

Have you guessed what it could be?
Look below and you will see,
It is...

Answer: A video game.

Lewis Hay (5)
St Mungo's Primary School & Nursery Class, Glasgow

Henry's First Riddle

What could it be?
Follow the clues and see.

It looks **delicious**.
It sounds **windy outside**.
It smells **like chocolate**.
It feels **hot**.
It tastes **like marshmallows**.

Have you guessed what it could be?
Look below and you will see,
It is...

Answer: *Hot chocolate.*

Henry Cogger (5)
Ysgol Bodafon, Llandudno

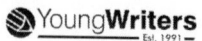

Stori-Mae's First Riddle

What could it be?
Follow the clues and see.

It looks **scaly**.
It sounds **loud**.
It smells **bad**.
It feels **soft**.

Have you guessed what it could be?
Look below and you will see,
It is...

Answer: A wolf.

Stori-Mae Paterson (5)
Ysgol Bodafon, Llandudno

YOUNG WRITERS INFORMATION

We hope you have enjoyed reading this book – and that you will continue to in the coming years.

If you're a young writer who enjoys reading and creative writing, or the parent of an enthusiastic poet or story writer, do visit our website **www.youngwriters.co.uk**. Here you will find free competitions, workshops and games, as well as recommended reads, a poetry glossary and our blog. There's lots to keep budding writers motivated to write!

If you would like to order further copies of this book, or any of our other titles, then please give us a call or order via your online account.

Young Writers
Remus House
Coltsfoot Drive
Peterborough
PE2 9BF
(01733) 890066
info@youngwriters.co.uk

Join in the conversation!
Tips, news, giveaways and much more!

Layla's First Riddle

What could it be?
Follow the clues and see.

It looks **yummy**.
It sounds **cosy**.
It smells **chocolatey**.
It feels **warm**.
It tastes **like chocolate**.

Have you guessed what it could be?
Look below and you will see,
It is...

Answer: *Hot chocolate.*

Layla Fairbairn-Percival (4)
Ysgol Bodafon, Llandudno